Americana Classics

Arranged by Marty Gross

Preface

There are few things more enjoyable than gathering with friends and family to make music together. This collection of songs has been designed to help make that experience easier. The music for each song displays the chord diagrams for five instruments: ukulele, baritone ukulele, guitar, mandolin, and banjo. The chord diagrams indicate basic, commonly used finger positions. More advanced players can substitute alternate chord formations.

The selections in this book are traditional American folksongs, modern folksongs and country classics. It is easy to find recordings of all these tunes by well-known artists including Pete Seeger, Joan Baez, Johnny Cash, Bob Dylan, Woody Guthrie, and Willie Nelson. Listening to these classic versions is a great way to gain an understanding of the traditional styles associated with these iconic songs.

- Marty Gross

ISBN 978-1-4803-5363-3

HAL•LEONARD®
CORPORATION
7777 W. BLUEMOUND RD. P.O. BOX 13819 MILWAUKEE, WI 53213

Visit Hal Leonard Online at
www.halleonard.com

Tuning

When you play with other musicians it is important that your instrument is in tune, not only with itself but also with the other players in the group. It may be helpful to choose one instrument in the group that you will all match your pitches to in order arrive at common tuning.

Learning to hear pitches and tuning by ear are important basic skills that every musician needs to develop. Electronic tuners can be a useful tool to help you check your tuning. Practice tuning by ear first, then check your pitches against the tuner. As time goes on you will find that your ability to tune by ear will become more and more accurate.

Good musicians are constantly adjusting the tuning of their instruments. During a playing session, continue to listen carefully and take the time to make adjustments when they are needed.

Soprano, Concert and Tenor Ukulele

Soprano, concert and tenor ukuleles all use the same standard tuning, also called "C tuning".

Some tenor players opt to replace the G string with a heavier gauge string tuned to the G an octave lower. Although the sound will be slightly different in color, the chord formations remain the same.

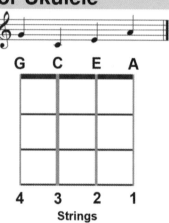

Baritone Ukulele

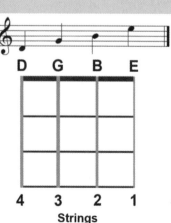

Baritone ukulele uses "G tuning". This is the same as the pitches used on the four highest strings of a guitar.

Guitar

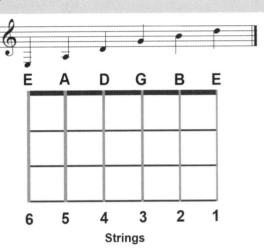

Guitar uses standard tuning throughout this book. The use of a capo has been avoided in order to accommodate the other instruments when playing together. If only guitars are being played, a capo can be added to adjust the singing range of any song.

Mandolin

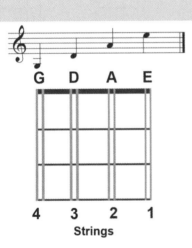

Standard tuning is used for all mandolin chord diagrams in this book.

Banjo

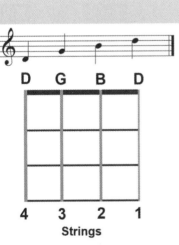

All banjo chord formations illustrated in this book are based on "Open G" tuning. If an alternate tuning is used, the banjo player can read the chord letters for the songs and disregard the diagrams.

Standard Ukulele

G  G7  C 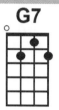 Em  D7

Baritone Ukulele

G  G7  C 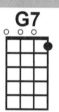 Em  D7

Guitar

G 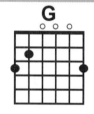 G7  C 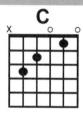 Em 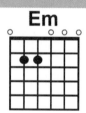 D7

Mandolin

G  G7 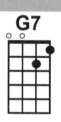 C  Em 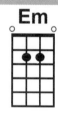 D7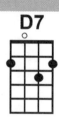

Banjo

G 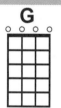 G7 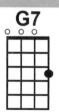 C  Em  D7

Amazing Grace

Words by John Newton
Traditional American Melody

Verse

1. A - maz - ing grace, how sweet the sound, that
   grace that taught my heart to fear, and
   man - y dan - gers, toils, and snares
   we've been there ten thou - sand years,

saved a wretch like me! I once was
grace my fears re - lieved; how once pre - cious
have al - read - y come; 'twas grace that
shin - ing as the sun, we've no less

lost but now am found; was blind, but now I
did that now grace ap - pear the hour I first be -
brought me safe thus far, and grace will lead me
days to sing God's praise than when we'd first be -

1., 2., 3.
see.
lieved.
home.

4.
2. 'Twas gun.
3. Through
4. When

Standard Ukulele

 G 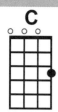 C 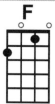 D7  F

Baritone Ukulele

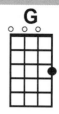 G  C  D7  F

Guitar

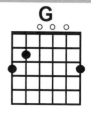 G 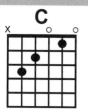 C  D7 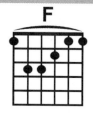 F

Mandolin

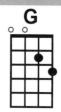 G 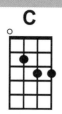 C 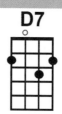 D7 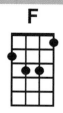 F

Banjo

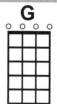 G 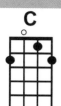 C 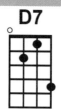 D7  F

Angels from Montgomery

Words and Music by John Prine

Verse

1. I am an old wom-an named af-ter my moth-er,
2. When I was a young girl I had me a cow-boy.
3. There's flies in the kitch-en, I can hear 'em there buzz-ing.

my old man is an-oth-er child that's grown old.
He weren't much to look at; free ram-blin' man.
And I ain't done noth-ing since I woke up to-day.

If dreams were light-ning, thun-der were de-sire,
But that was a long time; no mat-ter how I try,
How the hell can a per-son go to work in the morn-ing

this old house would have burnt down a long time a go.
the years just pass by like a bro-ken down dam.
and come home in the eve-ning and have noth-ing to say?

Chorus

Make me an an-gel that flies from Mont-gom-'ry, make me a post-er of an

old ro-de-o. Just give me one thing that I can hold on to;

to be-lieve in this liv-ing is just a hard way to go. go.

Standard Ukulele

D    G 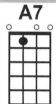   A7   Bm

Baritone Ukulele

D 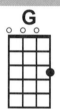   G    A7 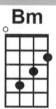   Bm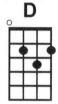

Guitar

D 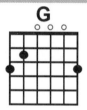   G    A7 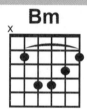   Bm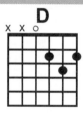

Mandolin

D    G    A7    Bm

Banjo

D 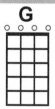   G    A7    Bm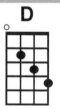

Blowin' in the Wind

Words and Music by Bob Dylan

Standard Ukulele

D7

G
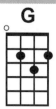

Baritone Ukulele

D7
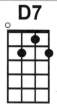

G
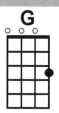

Guitar

D7
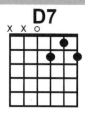

G
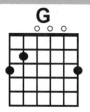

Mandolin

D7
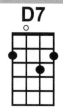

G
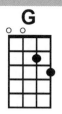

Banjo

D7
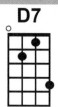

G
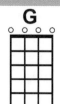

Chug-A-Lug

Words and Music by Roger Miller

Standard Ukulele

G 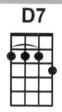 D7 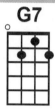 G7  C

Baritone Ukulele

G 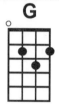 D7 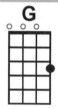 G7  C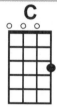

Guitar

G 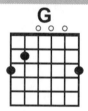 D7 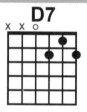 G7  C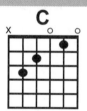

Mandolin

G  D7 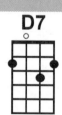 G7  C

Banjo

G 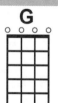 D7  G7 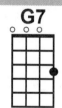 C

Cindy

Southern Appalachian Folksong

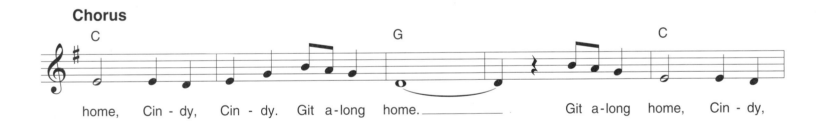

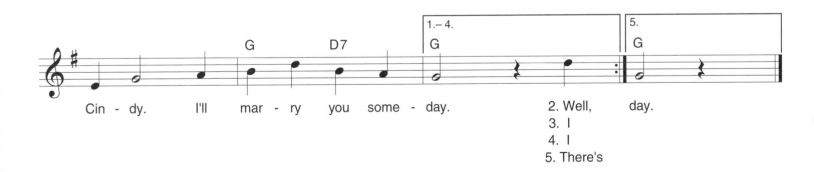

Standard Ukulele

C	G	Am	F	Em	D	Bb
		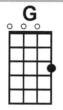		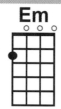		

Baritone Ukulele

C	G	Am	F	Em	D	Bb
	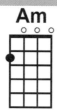		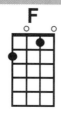		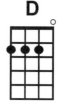	

Guitar

C	G	Am	F	Em	D	Bb
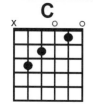	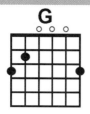	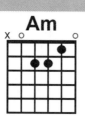	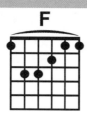	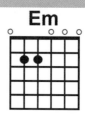	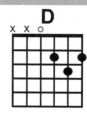	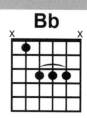

Mandolin

C	G	Am	F	Em	D	Bb
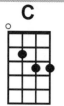	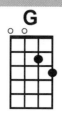	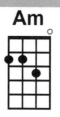				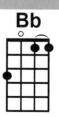

Banjo

C	G	Am	F	Em	D	Bb
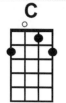	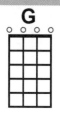			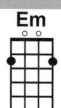	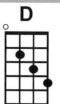	

City of New Orleans

Words and Music by Steve Goodman

www.stevegoodman.net

Standard Ukulele

G   D7   G7   C   C7

   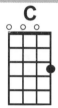 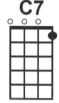

Baritone Ukulele

G   D7   G7   C   C7

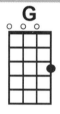 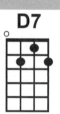   

Guitar

G   D7   G7   C   C7

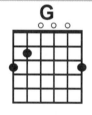  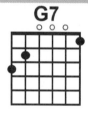 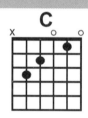 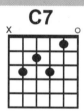

Mandolin

G   D7   G7   C   C7

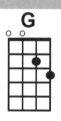 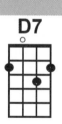   

Banjo

G   D7   G7   C   C7

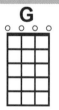  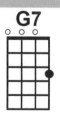  

The Crawdad Song

Traditional

Verse

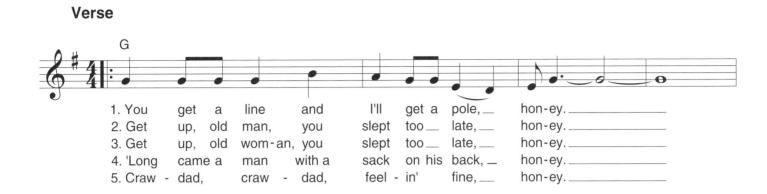

1. You get a line and I'll get a pole, __ hon-ey. __
2. Get up, old man, you slept too __ late, __ hon-ey. __
3. Get up, old wom-an, you slept too __ late, __ hon-ey. __
4. 'Long came a man with a sack on his back, __ hon-ey. __
5. Craw - dad, craw - dad, feel - in' fine, __ hon-ey. __

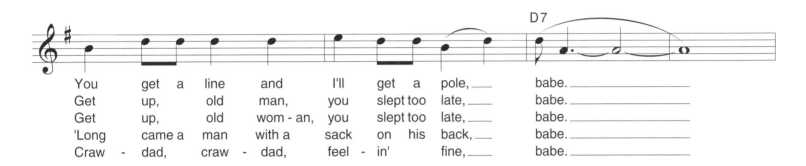

You get a line and I'll get a pole, __ babe. __
Get up, old man, you slept too late, __ babe. __
Get up, old wom - an, you slept too late, __ babe. __
'Long came a man with a sack on his back, __ babe. __
Craw - dad, craw - dad, feel - in' fine, __ babe. __

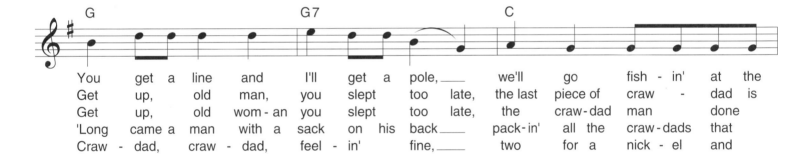

You get a line and I'll get a pole, ___ we'll go fish - in' at the
Get up, old man, you slept too late, the last piece of craw - dad is
Get up, old wom - an you slept too late, the craw-dad man done
'Long came a man with a sack on his back ___ pack-in' all the craw-dads that
Craw - dad, craw - dad, feel - in' fine, ___ two for a nick - el and

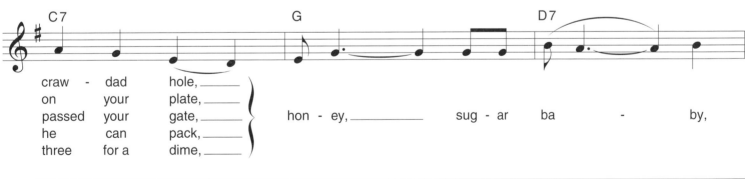

craw - dad hole, ___ } hon - ey, ___ sug - ar ba - by,
on your plate, ___ }
passed your gate, ___ }
he can pack, ___ }
three for a dime, ___ }

1.–4.
mine. ___

5.
mine. ___

Standard Ukulele

F  C 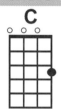 Dm 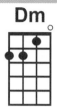 Bb  C7 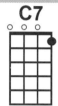 G7 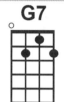 Am

Baritone Ukulele

F  C  Dm  Bb  C7  G7  Am

Guitar

F 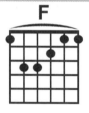 C 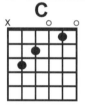 Dm 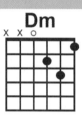 Bb 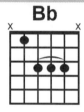 C7  G7  Am

Mandolin

F  C 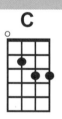 Dm  Bb  C7 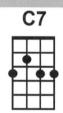 G7  Am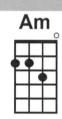

Banjo

F  C 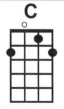 Dm 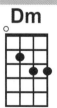 Bb  C7 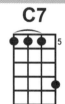 G7 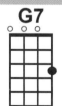 Am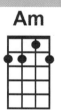

Don't Think Twice, It's All Right

Words and Music by Bob Dylan

Standard Ukulele

G  D  C 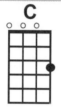 D7

Baritone Ukulele

G 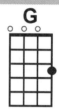 D  C  D7

Guitar

G 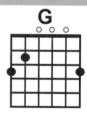 D 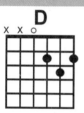 C 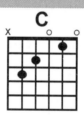 D7

Mandolin

G  D  C 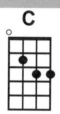 D7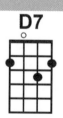

Banjo

G 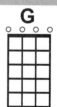 D 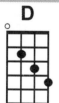 C 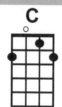 D7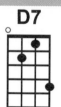

Down to the River to Pray

Traditional

Verse

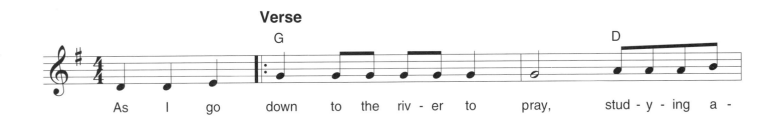

As I go down to the riv - er to pray, stud - y - ing a -

bout the good old way and who will wear the star - ry crown, oh Lord,

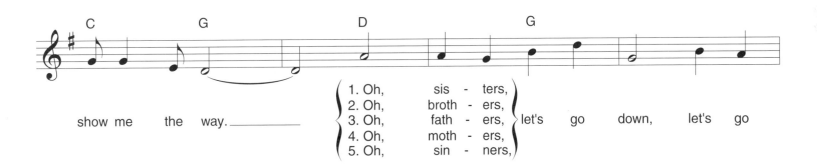

show me the way. _____

{
1. Oh, sis - ters,
2. Oh, broth - ers,
3. Oh, fath - ers, } let's go down, let's go
4. Oh, moth - ers,
5. Oh, sin - ners,
}

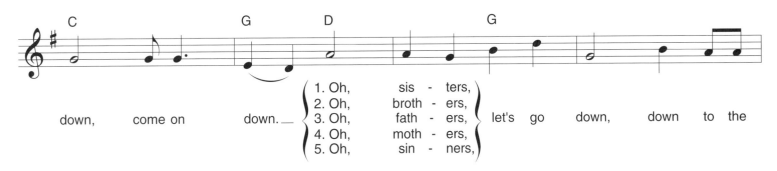

down, come on down. _

{
1. Oh, sis - ters,
2. Oh, broth - ers,
3. Oh, fath - ers, } let's go down, down to the
4. Oh, moth - ers,
5. Oh, sin - ners,
}

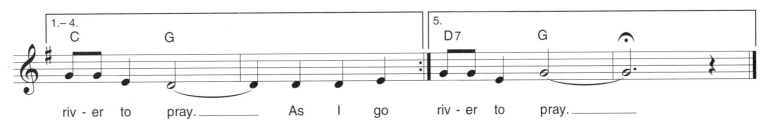

1.–4.
riv - er to pray. _____ As I go

5.
riv - er to pray. _____

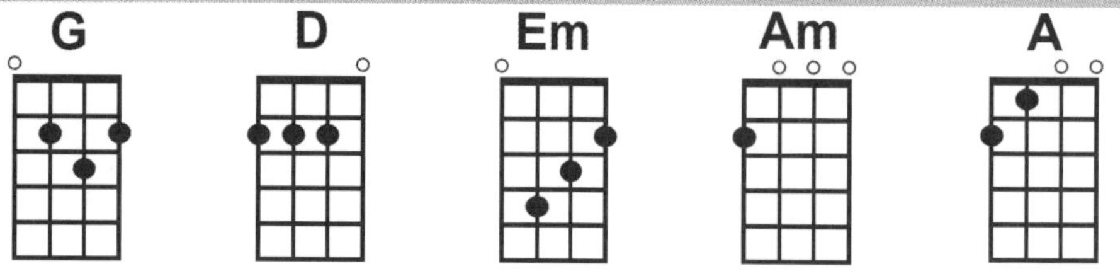

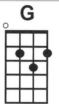

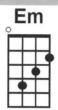

Standard Ukulele

G
D
Em
Am
A

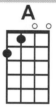

Baritone Ukulele

G
D
Em
Am
A

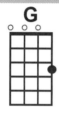

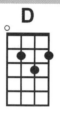

Guitar

G
D
Em
Am
A

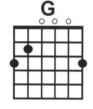

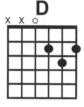

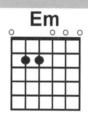

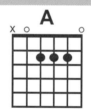

Mandolin

G
D
Em
Am
A

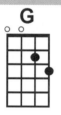

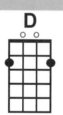

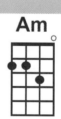

Banjo

G
D
Em
Am
A

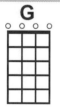

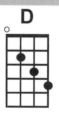

Dust in the Wind

Words and Music by Kerry Livgren

Standard Ukulele

G	C	Bm	Am7	D7	Em	A7
	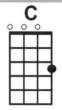		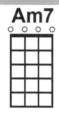			

Baritone Ukulele

G	C	Bm	Am7	D7	Em	A7
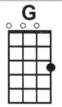		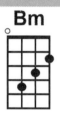				

Guitar

G	C	Bm	Am7	D7	Em	A7
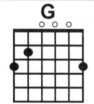	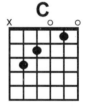	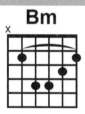	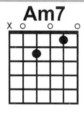		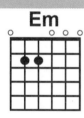	

Mandolin

G	C	Bm	Am7	D7	Em	A7
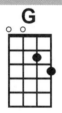	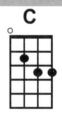		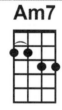		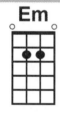	

Banjo

G	C	Bm	Am7	D7	Em	A7
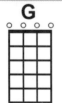		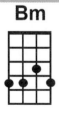			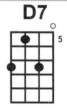	

Early in the Morning

Words and Music by Paul Stookey

Verse

Standard Ukulele

Dm	F	Gm	A7	Am	C7	C
						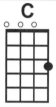

Baritone Ukulele

Dm	F	Gm	A7	Am	C7	C
		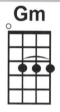				

Guitar

Dm	F	Gm	A7	Am	C7	C
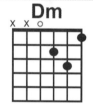			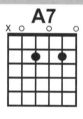	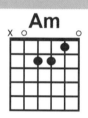	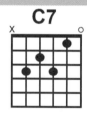	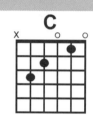

Mandolin

Dm	F	Gm	A7	Am	C7	C
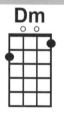						

Banjo

Dm	F	Gm	A7	Am	C7	C
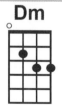		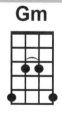				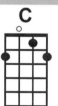

The Erie Canal
Traditional New York Work Song

Standard Ukulele

D   Bm   Em   G   A

 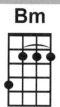 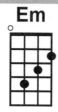  

Baritone Ukulele

D   Bm   Em   G   A

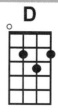   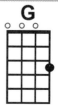 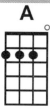

Guitar

D   Bm   Em   G   A

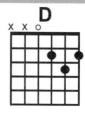 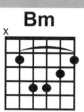 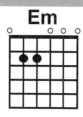  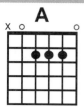

Mandolin

D   Bm   Em   G   A

 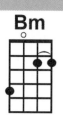  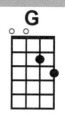 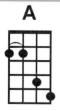

Banjo

D   Bm   Em   G   A

 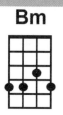  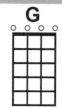 

Five Hundred Miles

Words and Music by Hedy West

Standard Ukulele

Em	A	G	D	Bm
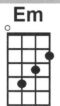	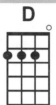			

Baritone Ukulele

Em	A	G	D	Bm
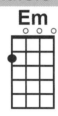		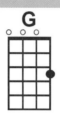	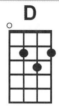	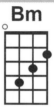

Guitar

Em	A	G	D	Bm
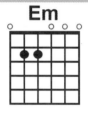	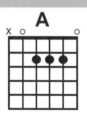	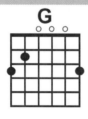	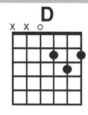	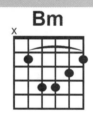

Mandolin

Em	A	G	D	Bm
	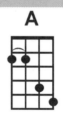		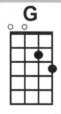	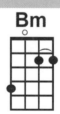

Banjo

Em	A	G	D	Bm
		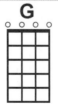		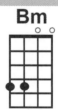

Follow the Drinkin' Gourd

African-American Spiritual

Standard Ukulele

G   C   D7

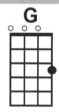  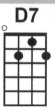

Baritone Ukulele

G   C   D7

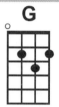 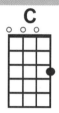 

Guitar

G   C   D7

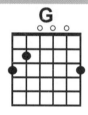 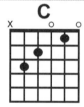 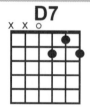

Mandolin

G   C   D7

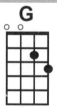 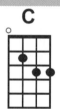 

Banjo

G   C   D7

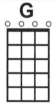  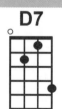

Folsom Prison Blues

Words and Music by John R. Cash

Standard Ukulele

| C | G7 | E7 | F |

 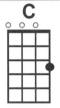  

Baritone Ukulele

| C | G7 | E7 | F |

 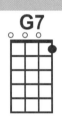  

Guitar

| C | G7 | E7 | F |

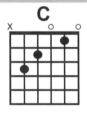  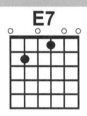 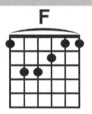

Mandolin

| C | G7 | E7 | F |

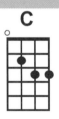   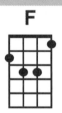

Banjo

| C | G7 | E7 | F |

 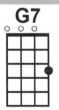  

Freight Train

Words and Music by Elizabeth Cotten

Standard Ukulele

D **G** **A7** **Bm7**

Baritone Ukulele

D 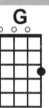 **G** **A7** **Bm7**

Guitar

D **G** **A7** **Bm7**

Mandolin

D **G** **A7** **Bm7**

Banjo

D **G** **A7** **Bm7**

Garden Song

Words and Music by Dave Mallett

Standard Ukulele

C   Dm   G7

  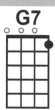

Baritone Ukulele

C   Dm   G7

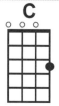  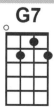

Guitar

C   Dm   G7

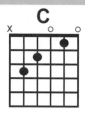 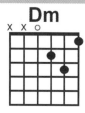 

Mandolin

C   Dm   G7

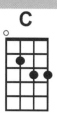  

Banjo

C   Dm   G7

 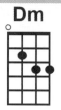 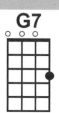

Gentle on My Mind

Words and Music by John Hartford

Verse

1. It's know-ing that your door is al-ways o-pen and your path is free to
cling-ing to the rocks and i-vy plan-ted on their col-umns now that
wheat fields and the clothes lines and the junk-yards and the high-ways come be-

walk, that makes me tend to leave my sleep-ing
binds me, or some-thin' that some-bod-y said be-
tween us, and some oth-er wom-an cry-in' to her

bag rolled up and stashed be-hind your couch. And it's
cause they thought we fit to-geth-er walk-in'. It's just
moth-er 'cause she turned and I was gone. And I

know-ing I'm not shack-led by for-got-ten words and bonds and the ink stains that have
know-ing that the world will not be curs-ing or for-giv-ing, when I walk a-long some
still might run in si-lence, tears of joy might stain my face and the sum-mer sun may

dried up-on some line, that keeps you in the
rail-road track and find that you're mov-ing by the
burn me 'til I'm blind but not to where I can

back roads by the riv-er of my mem-'ry, that keeps you ev-er gen-tle on my
back roads by the riv-er of my mem-'ries, and for hours you're just gen-tle on my
not see you walk-in' on the back roads by the riv-ers flow-ing gen-tle on my

1., 2. C

mind.
mind.

2. It's not

3. C

mind.

3. Though the

Standard Ukulele

G  **D7** 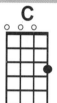 **C** 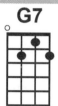 **G7**

Baritone Ukulele

G  **D7** 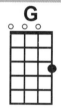 **C**  **G7**

Guitar

G 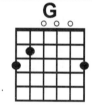 **D7**  **C** 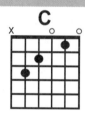 **G7**

Mandolin

G 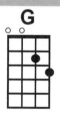 **D7**  **C** 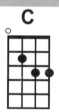 **G7**

Banjo

G 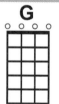 **D7** 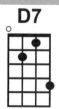 **C**  **G7**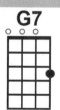

Goodnight, Irene

Words and Music by Huddie Ledbetter and John A. Lomax

Chorus

I - rene, good - night, _____ I - rene, good - night. _____ Good-

night, I - rene, good - night, I - rene, I'll see you in my dreams. _____

Verse

1. Sat - ur - day night I got mar - ried, _____ me and my
2. Some - times I live in the coun - try, _____ some - times I
3. Stop ram - blin', and stop your gam - blin', _____ stop stay - ing out

wife set - tled down. _____ Now me and my wife _____ are
live in the town, _____ and some - times I have a great
late at _____ night. _____ Go home to your wife and your

part - ed, _____ I'm gon - na take an - oth - er walk down -
no - tion _____ to _____ jump in - to the riv - er and
fam - 'ly, _____ sit _____ down by the fire - side

1., 2.
town. _____
drown. _____

3. *Repeat Chorus*
bright. _____

Standard Ukulele

C   C7   F   G7

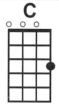   

Baritone Ukulele

C   C7   F   G7

   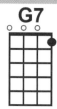

Guitar

C   C7   F   G7

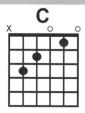 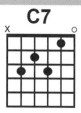 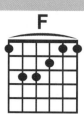 

Mandolin

C   C7   F   G7

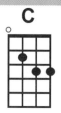   

Banjo

C   C7   F   G7

   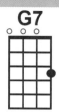

Hesitation Blues

Words and Music by Billy Smythe and J. Scott Middleton

Verse

1. I was born in Eng - land, raised in France. They'd
riv - er were whis - key and I was a duck, I'd
born in Al - a - bam - a, raised in Ten - nes - see. If
looked down the road as far as I can see. I've

send me the coat - hang - er but they would - n't send the pants.
dive down to the bot - tom and I'd nev - er come back up.
you don't want my peach - es don't you shake my tree.
got no wom - an, boys, so the blues have got me.
Oh,

Chorus

ba - by, how long will I have to wait?

Can I get you now, or must I hes - i -

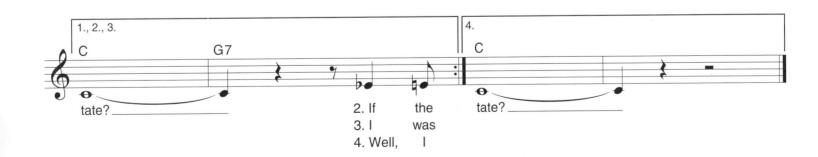

1., 2., 3.
tate?

4.
tate?

2. If the
3. I was
4. Well, I

Standard Ukulele

C	D7	G7	C7	F
	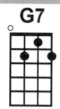			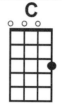

Baritone Ukulele

C	D7	G7	C7	F
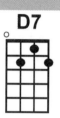	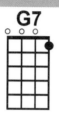			

Guitar

C	D7	G7	C7	F
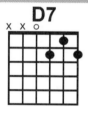	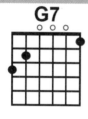	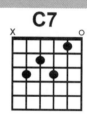	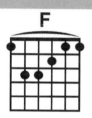	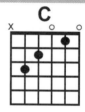

Mandolin

C	D7	G7	C7	F
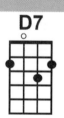			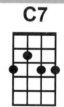	

Banjo

C	D7	G7	C7	F
	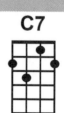		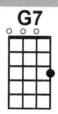	

Hey, Good Lookin'

Words and Music by Hank Williams

Standard Ukulele

Am	C	D	F	E	E7

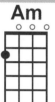    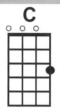 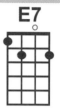

Baritone Ukulele

Am	C	D	F	E	E7

   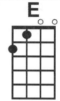  

Guitar

Am	C	D	F	E	E7

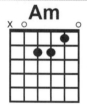 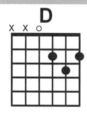  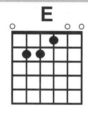 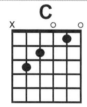 

Mandolin

Am	C	D	F	E	E7

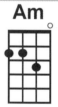     

Banjo

Am	C	D	F	E	E7

 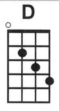    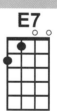

House of the Rising Sun

Southern American Folksong

Standard Ukulele

F  **Bb**  **C**  **C7**

Baritone Ukulele

F  **Bb**  **C**  **C7**

Guitar

F  **Bb** 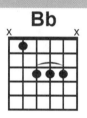 **C** 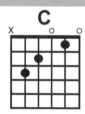 **C7**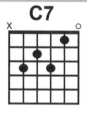

Mandolin

F  **Bb** 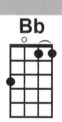 **C**  **C7**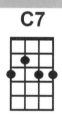

Banjo

F  **Bb** 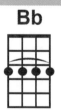 **C**  **C7**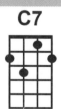

I Am a Man of Constant Sorrow

Words and Music by Carter Stanley

Standard Ukulele

D 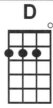 **A7**  **G**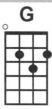

Baritone Ukulele

D  **A7**  **G**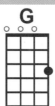

Guitar

D 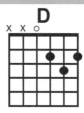 **A7**  **G**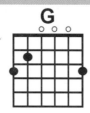

Mandolin

D  **A7** 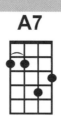 **G**

Banjo

D 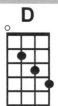 **A7** 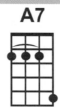 **G**

I Walk the Line

Words and Music by John R. Cash

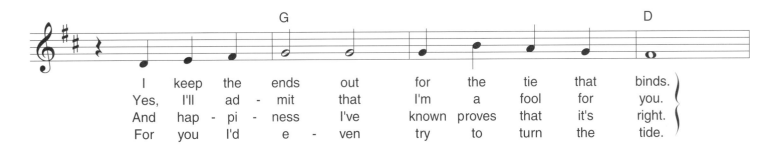

Standard Ukulele

G	B7	C	Em	D7	G7

  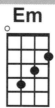

Baritone Ukulele

G	B7	C	Em	D7	G7

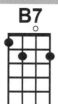  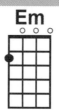  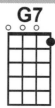

Guitar

G	B7	C	Em	D7	G7

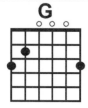 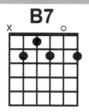 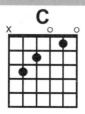 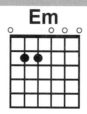 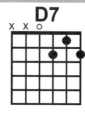 

Mandolin

G	B7	C	Em	D7	G7

  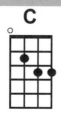   

Banjo

G	B7	C	Em	D7	G7

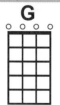 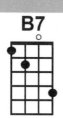  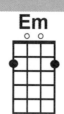  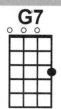

I'll Fly Away

Words and Music by Albert E. Brumley

Verse

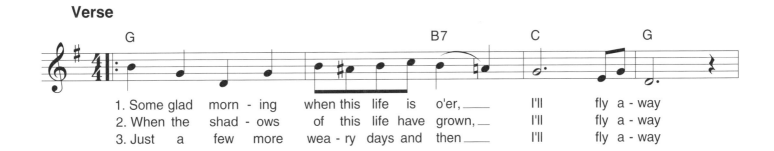

1. Some glad morn-ing when this life is o'er, ___ I'll fly a-way
2. When the shad-ows of this life have grown, ___ I'll fly a-way
3. Just a few more wea-ry days and then ___ I'll fly a-way

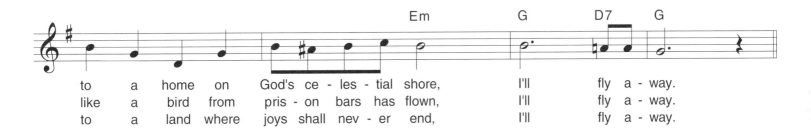

to a home on God's ce-les-tial shore, I'll fly a-way.
like a bird from pris-on bars has flown, I'll fly a-way.
to a land where joys shall nev-er end, I'll fly a-way.

Chorus

I'll fly a-way, o glo-ry, I'll fly a-way.

When I die hal-le-lu-jah by and by, I'll fly a-way. way.

Standard Ukulele

C 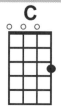 Em 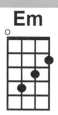 F  G  Am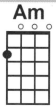

Baritone Ukulele

C  Em  F  G 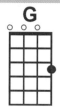 Am

Guitar

C 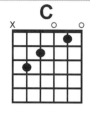 Em 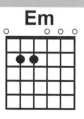 F 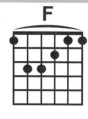 G 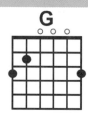 Am

Mandolin

C 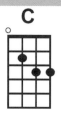 Em 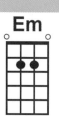 F  G  Am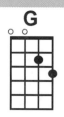

Banjo

C  Em  F  G 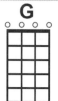 Am

56

If I Had a Hammer
(The Hammer Song)

Words and Music by Lee Hays and Pete Seeger

Standard Ukulele

D  G  E  A7

Baritone Ukulele

D 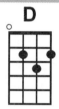 G  E 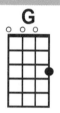 A7

Guitar

D 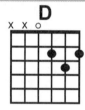 G 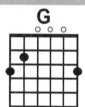 E 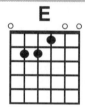 A7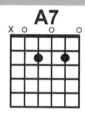

Mandolin

D  G 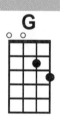 E  A7

Banjo

D  G 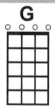 E  A7

In the Jailhouse Now

Words and Music by Jimmie Rogers

Standard Ukulele

C    G7

Baritone Ukulele

C    G7

Guitar

C 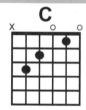   G7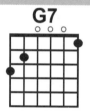

Mandolin

C 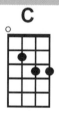   G7

Banjo

C    G7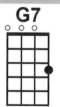

Jambalaya
(On the Bayou)

Words and Music by Hank Williams

Standard Ukulele

Am    **E7**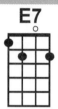

Baritone Ukulele

Am    **E7**

Guitar

Am    **E7**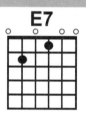

Mandolin

Am 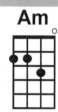   **E7**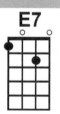

Banjo

Am   **E7**

Joshua (Fit the Battle of Jericho)

African-American Spiritual

Standard Ukulele

G   C   D7   A7   G7

 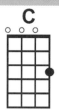   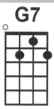

Baritone Ukulele

G   C   D7   A7   G7

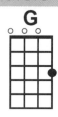  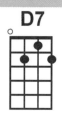  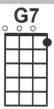

Guitar

G   C   D7   A7   G7

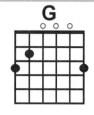 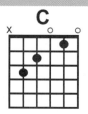 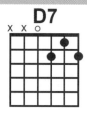 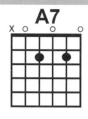 

Mandolin

G   C   D7   A7   G7

 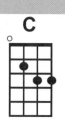  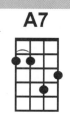 

Banjo

G   C   D7   A7   G7

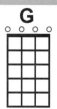    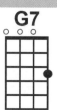

Keep on the Sunny Side

Words and Music by A.P. Carter

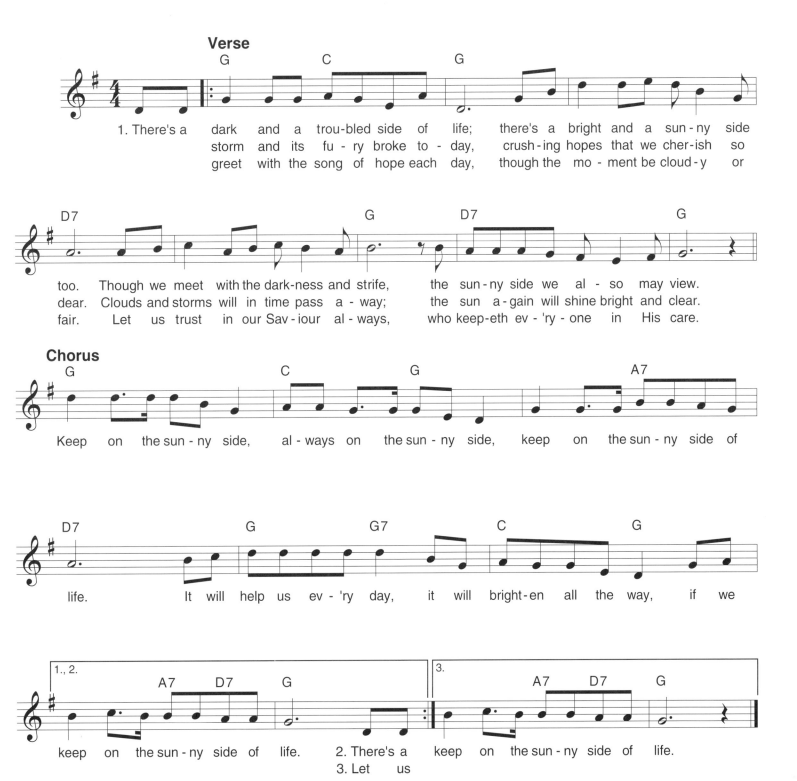

Standard Ukulele

G	C	D7	G7
	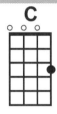		

Baritone Ukulele

G	C	D7	G7
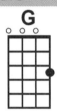	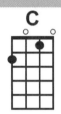		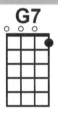

Guitar

G	C	D7	G7
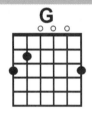	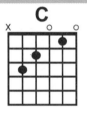		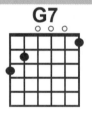

Mandolin

G	C	D7	G7
	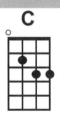	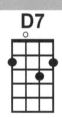	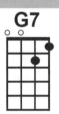

Banjo

G	C	D7	G7
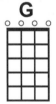			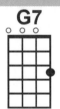

King of the Road

Words and Music by Roger Miller

Standard Ukulele

G   C 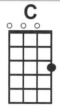 Em  D  D7  Am7

Baritone Ukulele

G 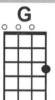 C 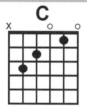 Em  D  D7  Am7

Guitar

G 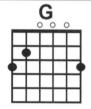 C 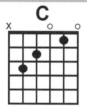 Em 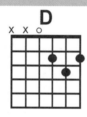 D 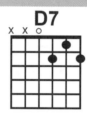 D7 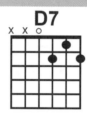 Am7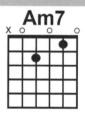

Mandolin

G 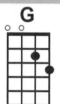 C  Em  D  D7  Am7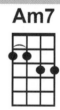

Banjo

G 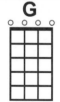 C  Em 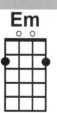 D 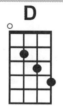 D7 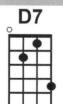 Am7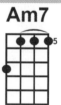

Leaving on a Jet Plane

Words and Music by John Denver

Verse

G

1. All my bags are packed,_ I'm read-y to go, I'm stand-ing here_ out-
man-y times_ I've let you down, so man-y times_ I've
3. Now the time_ has come to leave you, one more time_

C   G

side your door,_ I hate to wake_ you up to say_ good-bye._ But the
played a-round;_ I tell you now_ they don't mean_ a thing._ Ev-'ry
let me kiss_ you, close your eyes_ and I'll be on_ my way._

G   C   G   C

dawn is break-ing it's ear-ly morn,_ the tax-i's wait-in', he's blow-in' his horn,_ al-
place I go _ I'll think of you,_ ev-'ry song I sing_ I'll sing for you._ When
Dream a-bout_ the days to come, when I won't have_ to leave you a-lone,_ a-

Chorus

G   Em   D   D7   G

read-y I'm so lone-some I could die._
I come back I'll bring your wed-ding ring._ So kiss me and
bout the time that I won't have to say:_

C   G   C   G   Em   D7

smile for me,_ tell me that_ you'll wait for me,_ hold me like_ you'll nev-er let me go._

G   C   G   C

_ 'Cause I'm leav-in' on a jet_ plane, don't know when I'll be back_ a-gain.

1., 2.
Am7   D7

3.
Am7   D7

G   C

_ Oh, babe, I hate to go._ 2. There's so go._ I'm

Outro

G   C   G   C   *Repeat and fade*

leav-in',
Leav-in', on a jet_ plane, don't know when I'll be back_ a-gain.

Standard Ukulele

G   Am   D7   C   Em   Am7   G7

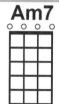

Baritone Ukulele

G   Am   D7   C   Em   Am7   G7

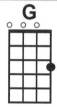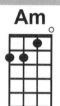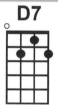

Guitar

G   Am   D7   C   Em   Am7   G7

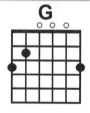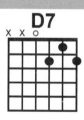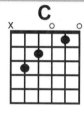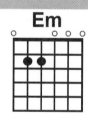

Mandolin

G   Am   D7   C   Em   Am7   G7

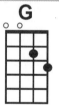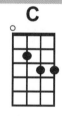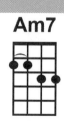

Banjo

G   Am   D7   C   Em   Am7   G7

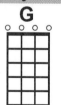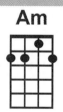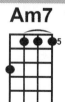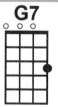

Lonesome Valley

New Words and New Music Adaption by Woody Guthrie

Standard Ukulele

G   **D**    **D7** 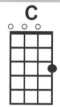   **C**    **G7** 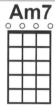   **Am7**

Baritone Ukulele

G 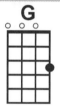   **D**    **D7**    **C**    **G7**    **Am7**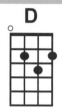

Guitar

G 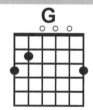   **D** 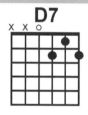   **D7** 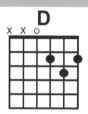   **C** 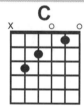   **G7**    **Am7**

Mandolin

G    **D**    **D7** 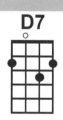   **C**    **G7** 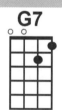   **Am7**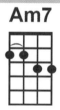

Banjo

G 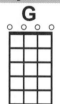   **D**    **D7** 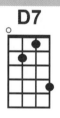   **C**    **G7** 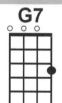   **Am7**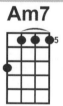

The Long Black Veil

Words and Music by Marijohn Wilkin and Danny Dill

Standard Ukulele

G7	C7	G	D7

Baritone Ukulele

G7	C7	G	D7

  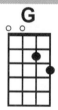 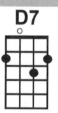

Guitar

G7	C7	G	D7

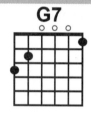 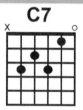 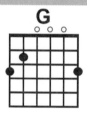 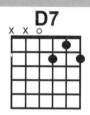

Mandolin

G7	C7	G	D7

 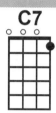  

Banjo

G7	C7	G	D7

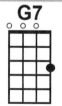 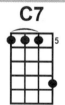 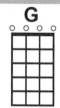 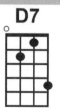

Midnight Special

Railroad Song

Standard Ukulele

C   C7   F   Fm   G7   Am   D7

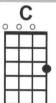 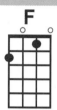   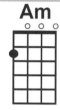 

Baritone Ukulele

C   C7   F   Fm   G7   Am   D7

    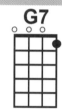  

Guitar

C   C7   F   Fm   G7   Am   D7

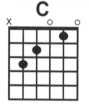 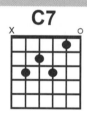 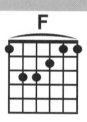    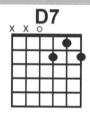

Mandolin

C   C7   F   Fm   G7   Am   D7

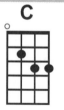 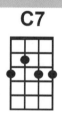    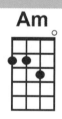 

Banjo

C   C7   F   Fm   G7   Am   D7

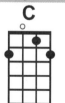    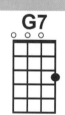  

Miss the Mississippi and You

Words and Music by Bill Halley

Standard Ukulele

C 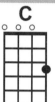 Em  Am 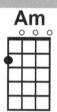 F  G 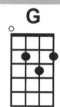 E7  D7

Baritone Ukulele

C  Em 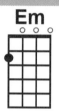 Am 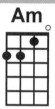 F  G  E7  D7

Guitar

C 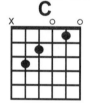 Em 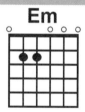 Am 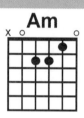 F 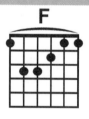 G  E7  D7

Mandolin

C 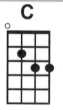 Em  Am  F  G  E7  D7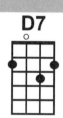

Banjo

C  Em  Am 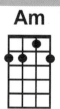 F  G  E7  D7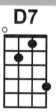

Mr. Bojangles

Words and Music by Jerry Jeff Walker

Standard Ukulele

G    C    A7 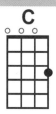   D7

Baritone Ukulele

G 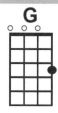   C    A7    D7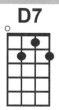

Guitar

G 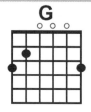   C 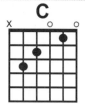   A7 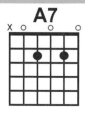   D7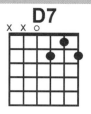

Mandolin

G    C    A7    D7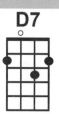

Banjo

G 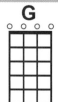   C    A7    D7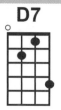

My Heroes Have Always Been Cowboys

Words and Music by Sharon Vaughn

Standard Ukulele

G **D7** **C**

  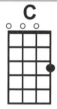

Baritone Ukulele

G **D7** **C**

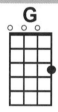  

Guitar

G **D7** **C**

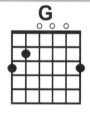  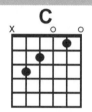

Mandolin

G **D7** **C**

 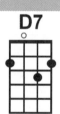 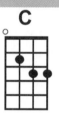

Banjo

G **D7** **C**

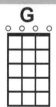 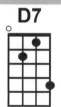 

My Home's Across the Blue Ridge Mountains

Traditional

Standard Ukulele

Em

G
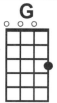

C

Am

D

D7

Baritone Ukulele

Em

G

C

Am
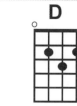

D
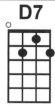

D7

Guitar

Em

G
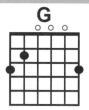

C
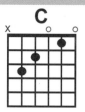

Am

D
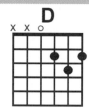

D7
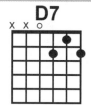

Mandolin

Em

G
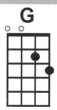

C
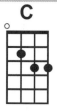

Am

D

D7
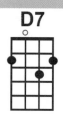

Banjo

Em

G
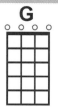

C
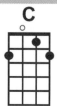

Am
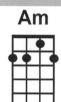

D
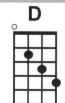

D7

The Night They Drove Old Dixie Down

Words and Music by Robbie Robertson

Standard Ukulele

G    G7 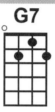   C    Em    D7

Baritone Ukulele

G 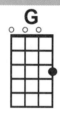   G7 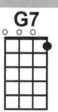   C    Em    D7

Guitar

G 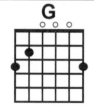   G7 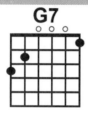   C 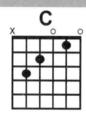   Em 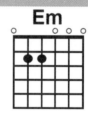   D7

Mandolin

G 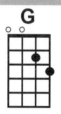   G7    C 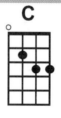   Em    D7

Banjo

G 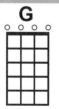   G7 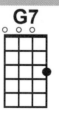   C    Em    D7

Oh Mary Don't You Weep

Traditional Spiritual

Standard Ukulele

G  D 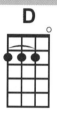 D7  C

Baritone Ukulele

G 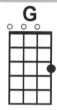 D 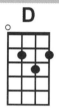 D7  C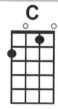

Guitar

G 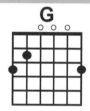 D 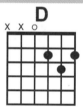 D7 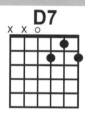 C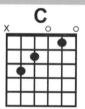

Mandolin

G  D  D7  C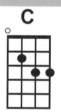

Banjo

G 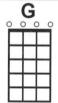 D  D7  C

Old Dan Tucker

Traditional

Verse

1. Old Dan Tuck-er is a fine old man. He washed his face in a
2. Old Dan Tuck-er is ___ come to town. He's rid-in' a goat and he's
3. Old Dan Tuck-er is ___ come to town. He's swing-in' the la - dies a -

fry - ing pan, combed his hair with a wag - on wheel,
lead-in' a hound. Hound dog barked and the bil - ly goat jumped,
round and round. First to the right and ___ then to the left,

Chorus

had a tooth - ache in his heel. Get out of the way, Old Dan Tuck-er,
land-ed Dan Tuck-er a - top a stump.
then to the girl that he likes best.

you're too late to get your sup-per. Sup-per's o - ver and break-fast's cook - in',

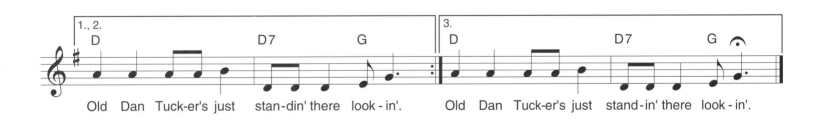

1., 2. Old Dan Tuck-er's just stan-din' there look - in'.

3. Old Dan Tuck-er's just stand-in' there look - in'.

Standard Ukulele

C 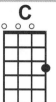 E7 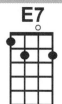 Dm  F  G7  C7

Baritone Ukulele

C  E7 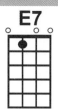 Dm 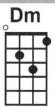 F  G7 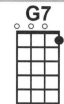 C7

Guitar

C 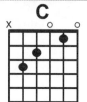 E7 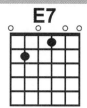 Dm 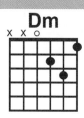 F  G7  C7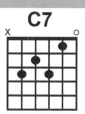

Mandolin

C 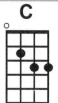 E7  Dm  F  G7  C7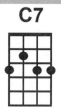

Banjo

C   E7  Dm 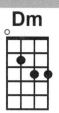 F  G7 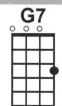 C7

On the Road Again

Words and Music by Willie Nelson

Standard Ukulele

C	F	G	G7
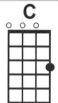			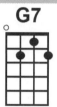

Baritone Ukulele

C	F	G	G7

Guitar

C	F	G	G7
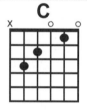	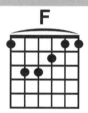		

Mandolin

C	F	G	G7
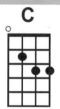			

Banjo

C	F	G	G7
		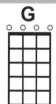	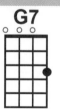

Pack Up Your Sorrows

Words and Music by Pauline Bryan and Richard Farina

Standard Ukulele

G	D7	G7	C
			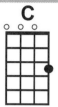

Baritone Ukulele

G	D7	G7	C
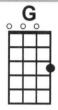		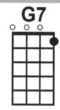	

Guitar

G	D7	G7	C
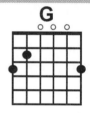	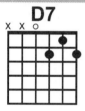		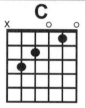

Mandolin

G	D7	G7	C
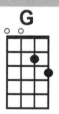	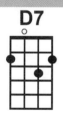	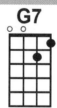	

Banjo

G	D7	G7	C
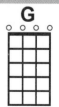	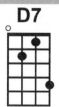		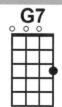

The Red River Valley

Traditional American Cowboy Song

Verse

1. From this val - ley they say you are go - ing;_____
   think of this val - ley you're leav - ing?_____
   long time, my dar - ling, I've wait - ed_____
   sit by my side if you love me._____

_____ we will miss your bright eyes and sweet smile,_____ for they
_____ Oh, how lone - ly, how sad it will be._____ Oh,_____
_____ for the sweet words you nev - er would say._____ Now, at
_____ Do not has - ten to bid me a - dieu,_____ but re -

say you are tak - ing the sun - shine_____ that has bright - ened our
think of the fond heart you're break - ing_____ and the grief you are
last, all my fond hopes have van - ished_____ for they say you are
mem - ber the Red Riv - er Val - ley_____ and the cow - boy that

| 1., 2., 3. | 4. |

path - way a - while._____ 2. Won't you true._____
caus - ing to me._____ 3. For a
go - ing a - way._____ 4. Come and
loves you so

Standard Ukulele

D	G	A	F#m	Em
			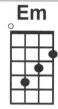	

Baritone Ukulele

D	G	A	F#m	Em
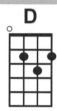	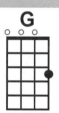	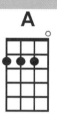	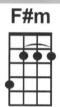	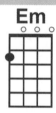

Guitar

D	G	A	F#m	Em
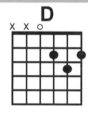	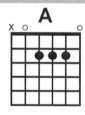			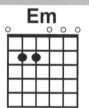

Mandolin

D	G	A	F#m	Em
	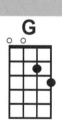			

Banjo

D	G	A	F#m	Em
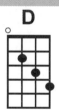	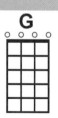			

River

Words and Music by Bill Staines

Standard Ukulele

G	A	D	C7	D7
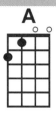		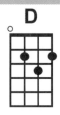		

Baritone Ukulele

G	A	D	C7	D7
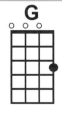	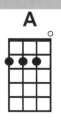	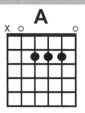	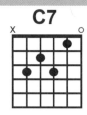	

Guitar

G	A	D	C7	D7
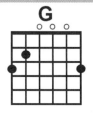	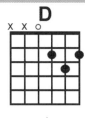	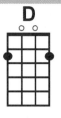		

Mandolin

G	A	D	C7	D7
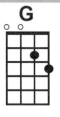		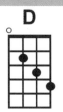	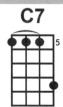	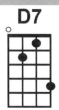

Banjo

G	A	D	C7	D7
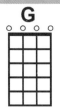			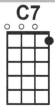	

Rock Island Line
Railroad Song

Chorus

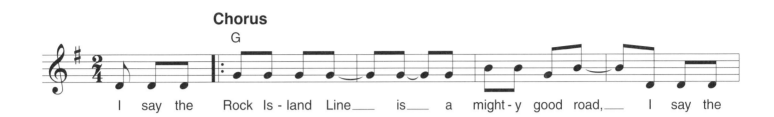

I say the Rock Is - land Line__ is__ a might - y good road,__ I say the

Rock Is - land Line__ is__ the road to ride. Oh, the Rock Is - land Line_

_ is a might - y good road.__ If__ you want__ to ride it got to

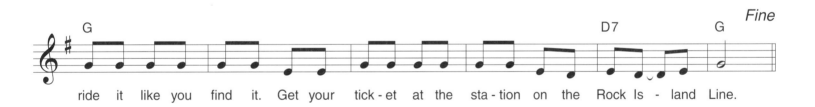

ride it like you find it. Get your tick - et at the sta - tion on the Rock Is - land Line.

Verse

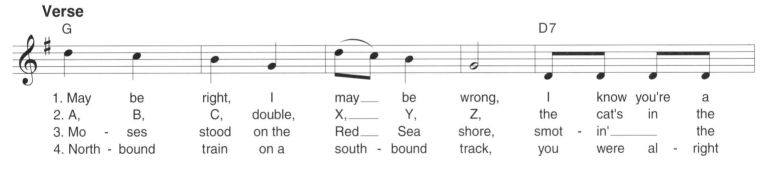

1. May be right, I may__ be wrong, I know you're a
2. A, B, C, double, X,__ Y, Z, the cat's in the
3. Mo - ses stood on the Red__ Sea shore, smot - in'__ the
4. North - bound train on a south - bound track, you were al - right

gon - na miss me when__ I'm gone. I say the   I say the
cup - board but he can't__ see me.
wa - ter with a two - by - four.
leav - in' but you won't__ be back.

Standard Ukulele

D	G	Bm	A7	A	C
			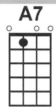	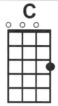	

Baritone Ukulele

D	G	Bm	A7	A	C
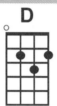	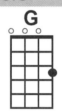				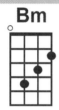

Guitar

D	G	Bm	A7	A	C
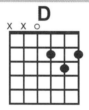	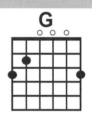	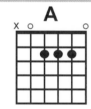	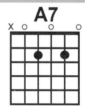	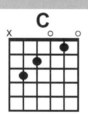	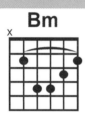

Mandolin

D	G	Bm	A7	A	C
		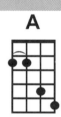	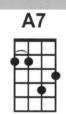		

Banjo

D	G	Bm	A7	A	C
	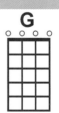				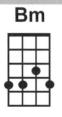

Rocky Top

Words and Music by Boudleaux Bryant and Felice Bryant

Verse

1. Wish that I was on ol' Rock-y Top, down in the Ten-nes-see hills;
2. Once two stran-gers climbed ol' Rock-y Top look-in' for a moon-shine still.

ain't no smog-gy smoke on Rock-y Top; ain't no tel-e-phone bills.
Stran-gers ain't come back from Rock-y Top; reck'n they nev-er will.

Corn won't grow at all on Rock-y Top, the dirt's too rock-y by far.
I've had years of cramped up cit-y life, trapped like a duck in a pen.

That's why all the folks on Rock-y Top get their corn from a jar.
All I know is it's a pit-y life can't be sim-ple a-gain.

Chorus

Rock-y Top will al-ways be home, sweet home to me; good ol' Rock-y Top,

Rock-y Top Ten-nes-see, Rock-y Top Ten-nes-see. Rock-y Top Ten-nes-see.

Standard Ukulele

Dm	C	Am
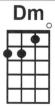	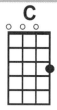	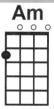

Baritone Ukulele

Dm	C	Am
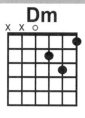	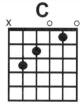	

Guitar

Dm	C	Am

Mandolin

Dm	C	Am
	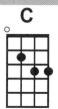	

Banjo

Dm	C	Am
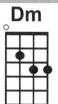		

Shady Grove

Appalachian Folk Song

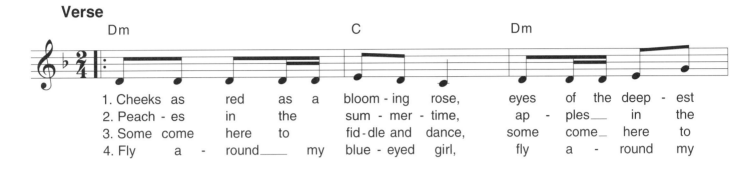

1. Cheeks as red as a bloom-ing rose, eyes of the deep-est
2. Peach-es in the sum-mer-time, ap-ples in the
3. Some come here to fid-dle and dance, some come here to
4. Fly a-round my blue-eyed girl, fly a-round my

brown; you are the dar-lin' of my heart.
fall; if I can't have the girl I love,
tar-ry, some come here to fid-dle and dance,
dai-sy, go fly a-round my blue-eyed girl,

Chorus

Stay 'til the sun goes down. Shad-y Grove,
won't have no girl at all.
I come here to mar-ry.
near-ly drive me cra-zy.

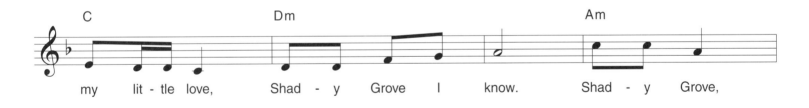

my lit-tle love, Shad-y Grove I know. Shad-y Grove,

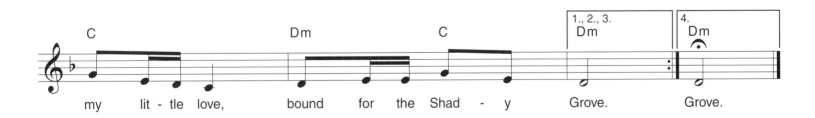

my lit-tle love, bound for the Shad-y Grove. Grove.

1., 2., 3. | 4.

Standard Ukulele

C  F 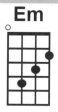 Em  Am  Fm  G7

Baritone Ukulele

C  F 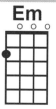 Em  Am  Fm  G7

Guitar

C 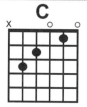 F 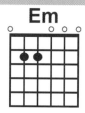 Em 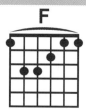 Am  Fm  G7

Mandolin

C 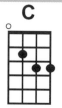 F  Em  Am  Fm  G7

Banjo

C  F 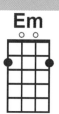 Em  Am  Fm 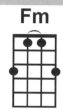 G7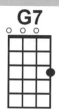

Shenandoah

American Folksong

Verse

1. Oh, Shen - an - doah, _____ I long to hear you, _____ a -
Shen - an - doah, _____ I love your daugh - ter, _____ a -
Shen - an - doah, _____ I'm bound to leave you, _____ a -

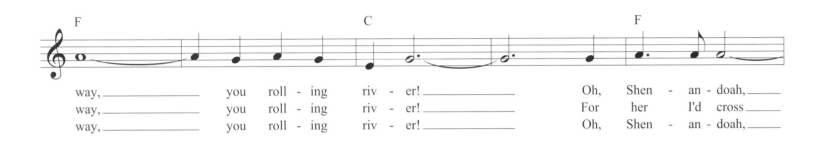

way, _____ you roll - ing riv - er! _____ Oh, Shen - an - doah,
way, _____ you roll - ing riv - er! _____ For her I'd cross _____
way, _____ you roll - ing riv - er! _____ Oh, Shen - an - doah, _____

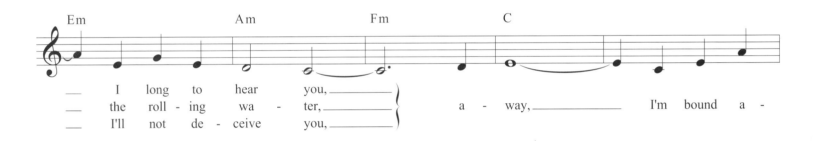

____ I long to hear you, _____ a - way, _____ I'm bound a -
____ the roll - ing wa - ter, _____
____ I'll not de - ceive you, _____

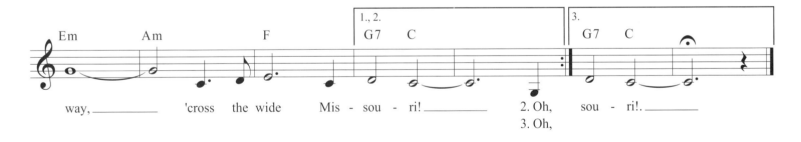

1., 2.
3.

way, _____ 'cross the wide Mis - sou - ri! _____ 2. Oh, sou - ri!.
3. Oh,

Standard Ukulele

Em	Em7	C	B7	Am	C7
	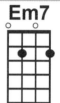				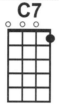

Baritone Ukulele

Em	Em7	C	B7	Am	C7
	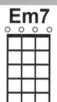				

Guitar

Em	Em7	C	B7	Am	C7
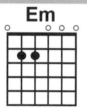	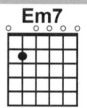	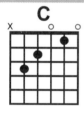	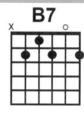	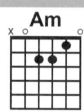	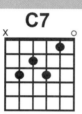

Mandolin

Em	Em7	C	B7	Am	C7
	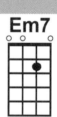	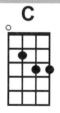			

Banjo

Em	Em7	C	B7	Am	C7
	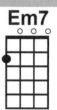	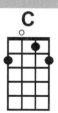			

Sixteen Tons

Words and Music by Merle Travis

Standard Ukulele

C 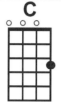 F  G7 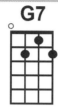 C7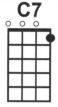

Baritone Ukulele

C  F  G7  C7

Guitar

C 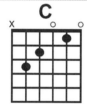 F 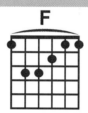 G7 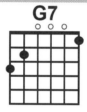 C7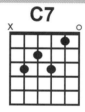

Mandolin

C 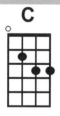 F  G7 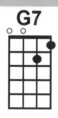 C7

Banjo

C  F  G7 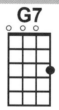 C7

So Long It's Been Good to Know Yuh
(Dusty Old Dust)

Words and Music by Woody Guthrie

Verse

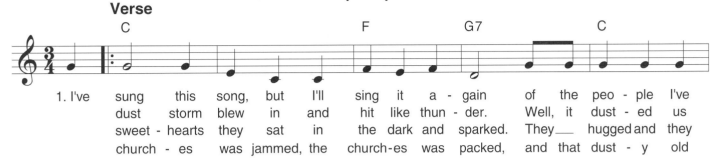

1. I've sung this song, but I'll sing it a-gain of the peo-ple I've
   dust storm blew in and hit like thun-der. Well, it dust-ed us
   sweet-hearts they sat in the dark and sparked. They___ hugged and they
   church-es was jammed, the church-es was packed, and that dust-y old

met and the plac-es I've been, of some of the trou-bles that both-ered my mind, and a-
o-ver and cov-ered us under. It blocked all the traf-fic and blocked out the sun. Right on
kissed in that dust-y old dark. They sighed and they cried and they hugged and they kissed, but in-
dust storm, it blowed on so black. The preach-er could not read a word of his text, so he

Chorus

lot of good peo-ple that I've left be-hind. Sing-ing
straight to their homes all the peo-ple did run, say-ing   so   long, it's been good_ to
stead of a mar-riage they talked a-bout this: Hon-ey,
fold-ed his specs, took the col-lec-tion and said,"Breth-ren,

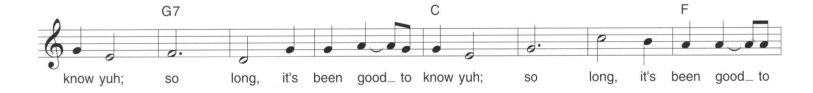

know yuh; so   long, it's been good_ to know yuh; so   long, it's been good_ to

know yuh. What a long   time_ since I've been home,___   and I have to be

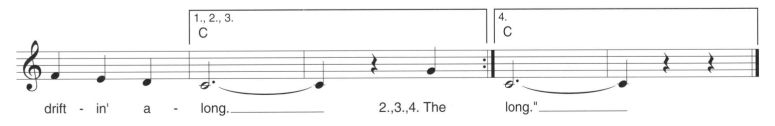

drift-in' a-long.___   2.,3.,4. The   long."___

Standard Ukulele

D    G    A7    D7

Baritone Ukulele

D    G    A7 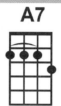   D7

Guitar

D 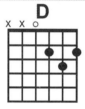   G    A7    D7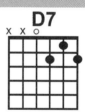

Mandolin

D    G 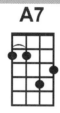   A7    D7

Banjo

D 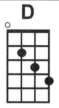   G    A7    D7

Swing Low, Sweet Chariot

Traditional Spiritual

Standard Ukulele

G	Em	D	C	F	D7

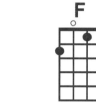

Baritone Ukulele

G	Em	D	C	F	D7

Guitar

G	Em	D	C	F	D7

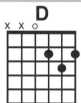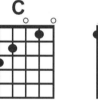

Mandolin

G	Em	D	C	F	D7

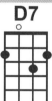

Banjo

G	Em	D	C	F	D7

Take Me Home, Country Roads

Words and Music by John Denver, Bill Danoff and Taffy Nivert

Standard Ukulele

 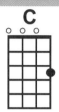   

Baritone Ukulele

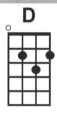  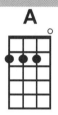  

Guitar

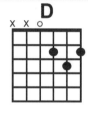 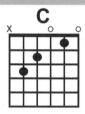 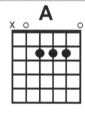  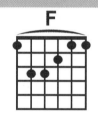

Mandolin

 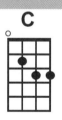  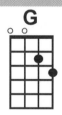 

Banjo

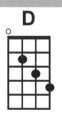   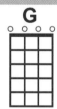 

Tennessee Stud

Words and Music by Jimmie Driftwood

Standard Ukulele

G	G7	C	E7	A7	D7	B7
				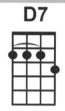		

Baritone Ukulele

G	G7	C	E7	A7	D7	B7
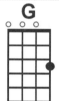					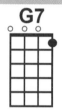	

Guitar

G	G7	C	E7	A7	D7	B7
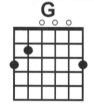	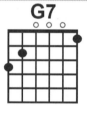	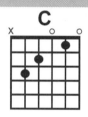	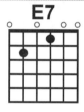			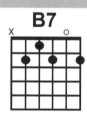

Mandolin

G	G7	C	E7	A7	D7	B7
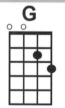				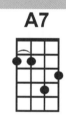		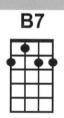

Banjo

G	G7	C	E7	A7	D7	B7
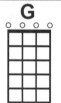	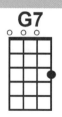		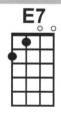			

Tennessee Waltz

Words and Music by Redd Stewart and Pee Wee King

Standard Ukulele

G	D	A7
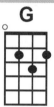	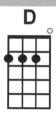	

Baritone Ukulele

G	D	A7
	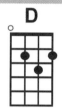	

Guitar

G	D	A7
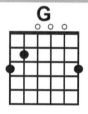	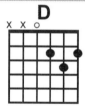	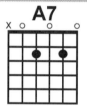

Mandolin

G	D	A7

Banjo

G	D	A7
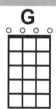		

This Land is Your Land

Words and Music by Woody Guthrie

Standard Ukulele

D	A7	D7	G	G7
			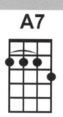	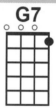

Baritone Ukulele

D	A7	D7	G	G7
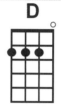			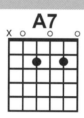	

Guitar

D	A7	D7	G	G7
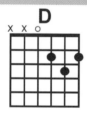	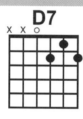	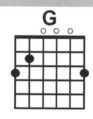		

Mandolin

D	A7	D7	G	G7
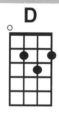	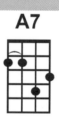			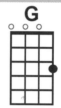

Banjo

D	A7	D7	G	G7
		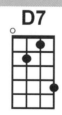	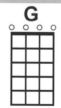	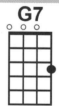

This Train

Traditional

Standard Ukulele

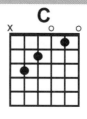 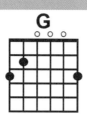   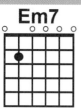

Baritone Ukulele

  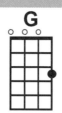  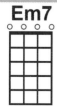

Guitar

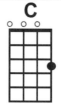  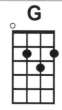 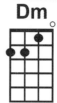 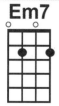

Mandolin

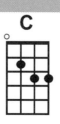 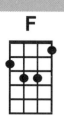 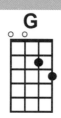  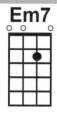

Banjo

  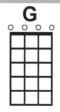 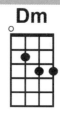 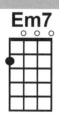

Turn! Turn! Turn!
(To Everything There Is a Season)

Words from the Book of Ecclesiastes
Adaptation and Music by Pete Seeger

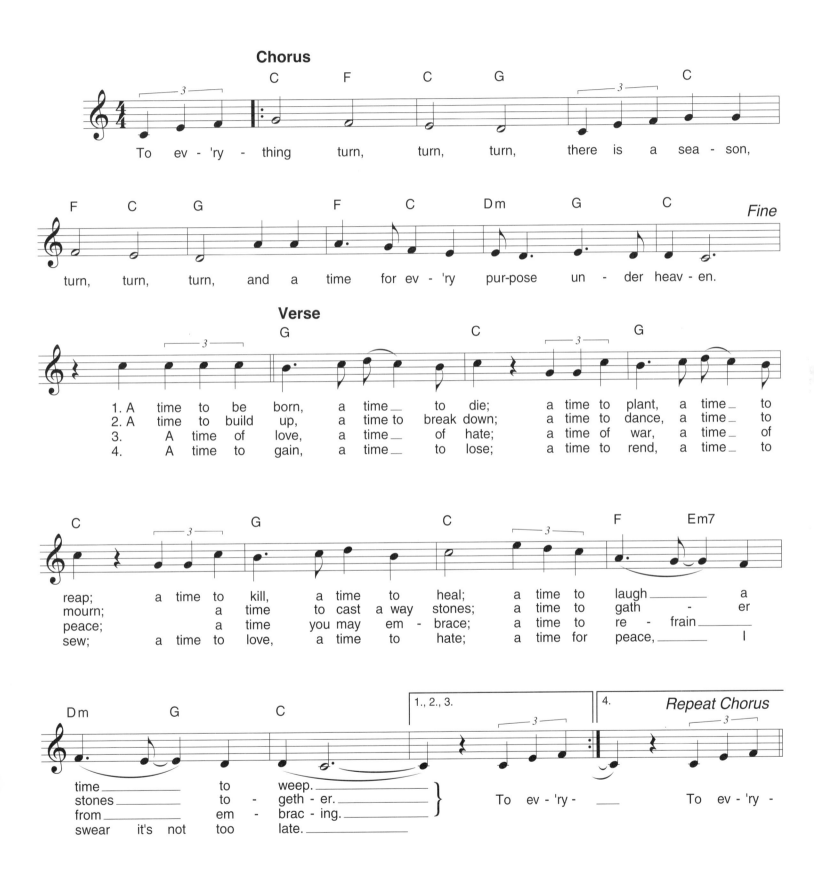

Standard Ukulele

D   **A7**  **G**  **Bb**

Baritone Ukulele

D  **A7**  **G** 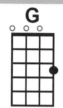 **Bb**

Guitar

D 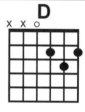 **A7** 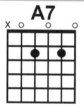 **G**  **Bb**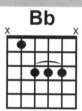

Mandolin

D  **A7** 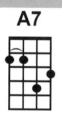 **G**  **Bb**

Banjo

D 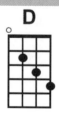 **A7**  **G** 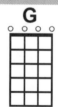 **Bb**

Wabash Blues

Words by Dave Ringel
Music by Fred Meinken

Standard Ukulele

G **C** **D7**

 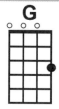 

Baritone Ukulele

G **C** **D7**

 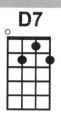 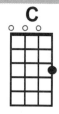

Guitar

G **C** **D7**

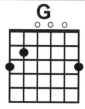 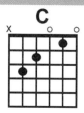 

Mandolin

G **C** **D7**

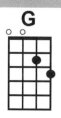  

Banjo

G **C** **D7**

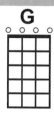  

The Wabash Cannon Ball

Hobo Song

Standard Ukulele

Dm 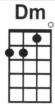 **A7**  **G7**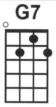

Baritone Ukulele

Dm  **A7** 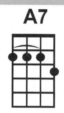 **G7**

Guitar

Dm 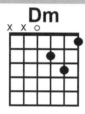 **A7** 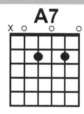 **G7**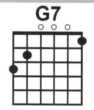

Mandolin

Dm  **A7**  **G7**

Banjo

Dm 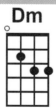 **A7**  **G7**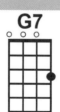

Wade in the Water

Traditional Spiritual

Chorus

Wade ___ in the wa - ter, ___ wade ___ in the wa - ter chil - dren,

Fine

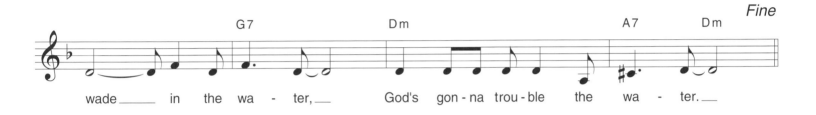

wade ___ in the wa - ter, ___ God's gon - na trou - ble the wa - ter.

Verse

1. Who are those chil - dren all dressed in red? ___
2. Who are those chil - dren all dressed in white? ___
3. Who are those chil - dren all dressed in blue? ___

God's gon - na trou - ble the

wa - ter. ___

It must be the ones that ___ Mos - es led. ___
It must be the chil - dren of the Is - ra - el - ites. ___
It must be the ones that ___ made it through. ___

1., 2.
A7   Dm

3.   *Repeat Chorus*
A7   Dm

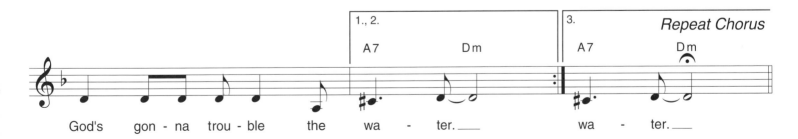

God's gon - na trou - ble the wa - ter. ___   wa - ter.

Standard Ukulele

G	D	Em	C
	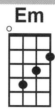	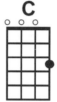	

Baritone Ukulele

G	D	Em	C
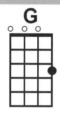	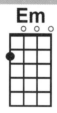		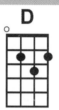

Guitar

G	D	Em	C
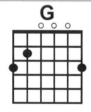	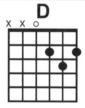	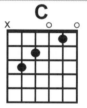	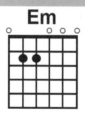

Mandolin

G	D	Em	C
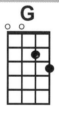		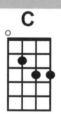	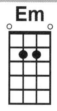

Banjo

G	D	Em	C
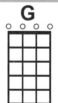	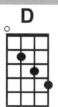		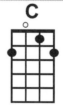

Wagon Wheel

Words and Music by Ketch Secor and Bob Dylan

Verse

1. Head - in' down south to the land of the pines, I'm thumb-in' my way to North
2. Run - nin' from the cold up in New Eng - land, I was born to be a fid-dler in an
3. Walk - in' through the South out of Ro - a-noake I caught a truck - er out of Phil-ly, had a

— Car-o - line. I'm star-in' up the road and pray to God I see head - lights.
— old time string band. My ba - by plays a gui-tar, I pick a ban-jo now.
nice long toke, but he's a head-in' west from the Cum-ber-land Gap to John - son Cit-y,

I made it to the coast in sev - en-teen hours. Pick-in' me a bou - quet of dog-
Oh, north coun-try win - ters keep get-tin' me down. Lost my mon - ey play-in' po - ker so I
Ten-nes-nee, I've got to get a move on be - fore the sun. I know my ba - by's wait-in' and I

— wood flow'rs and I'm a hop-in' for Ra - leigh, I can see my ba - by to - night.
had to leave town, I ain't turn - in' back to liv - in' that old life no more.
— know that she's the on - ly one and if I die in Ra - leigh, at least I will die free.

Chorus

So, rock me, ma-ma, like a wag-on wheel. Rock me, ma-ma, an - y way you feel.

Hey, ma - ma, rock me. Rock me, ma-ma, like the wind and the rain.

Rock me, ma - ma, like a south-bound train. Hey, ma - ma, rock me.

1., 2. *3.*

Hey, hey, ma - ma, rock me.

Standard Ukulele

G	C	Em	Am	D	D7	Bm
	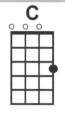		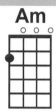	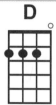	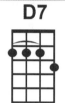	

Baritone Ukulele

G	C	Em	Am	D	D7	Bm
		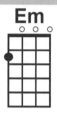		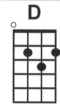		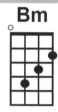

Guitar

G	C	Em	Am	D	D7	Bm
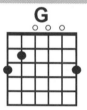	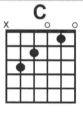	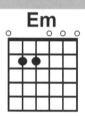		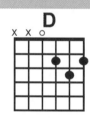		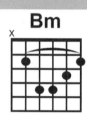

Mandolin

G	C	Em	Am	D	D7	Bm
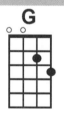					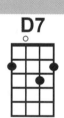	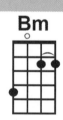

Banjo

G	C	Em	Am	D	D7	Bm
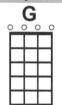			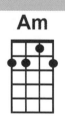		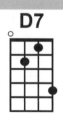	

Water Is Wide

Traditional

Verse

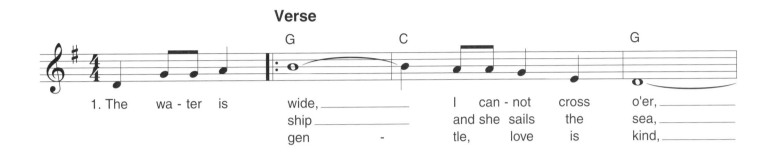

1. The wa-ter is wide, _____ I can-not cross o'er, _____
ship _____ and she sails the sea, _____
gen - tle, love is kind, _____

___ and neith-er have _____ I wings to fly. _____ Build me a
___ she's load-ed deep, _____ as deep can be. _____ But not so
___ fresh as a flow'r _____ when first it's new. _____ But love grows

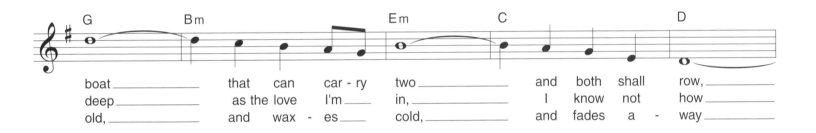

boat _____ that can car-ry two _____ and both shall row, _____
deep _____ as the love I'm in, _____ I know not how
old, _____ and wax - es _____ cold, and fades a - way

___ my love and I. _____ 2. There is a dew. _____
___ to sink or swim. _____ 3. Oh, love is
___ like morn - ing

Standard Ukulele

G   Bm   C   D

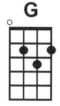  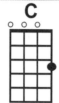 

Baritone Ukulele

G   Bm   C   D

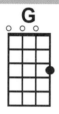   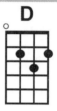

Guitar

G   Bm   C   D

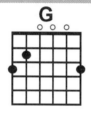  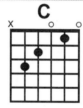 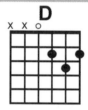

Mandolin

G   Bm   C   D

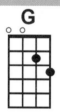   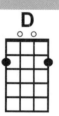

Banjo

G   Bm   C   D

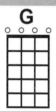   

The Weight

By J.R. Robertson

Verse

1. I pulled in - to Naz - a - reth, was feel-in' 'bout half - past dead.
2. I picked up my bag, and I went look-in' for a place to hide
3. Cra - zy Ches - ter fol - lowed me and caught me in the fog.
4. Get your Can - non - ball now to take me down the line.

I just need some - place where I can lay my head.
when I saw old Car - men and the dev - il walk - in' side by side.
He said, "I will fix your rack if you'll take Jack, my dog.
My bag is sink - in' low, and I do be - lieve it's time

"Hey, mis - ter can you tell me where a man might find a bed?"
So I said, "Hey, Car - men, let's go down - town."
I said, "Wait a min - ute, Ches - ter, you know I'm a peace - ful man."
to get back to Miss Fan - ny. You know, she's the on - ly one

He just grinned and shook my hand, "No" is all he said.
Car - men said, "I got - ta go, but my friend can stick a - round."
He said, "Boy, that's o - kay. Won't you feed him when you can?"
who sent me here with her re - gards for ev - 'ry one.

Chorus

Take a load off, Fan - ny, take a load for free. Take a load off, Fan - ny,

and you put the load right on me.

me.

Copyright © 1968, 1974 (Renewed) Dwarf Music
International Copyright Secured All Rights Reserved
Reprinted by Permission of Music Sales Corporation

135

Standard Ukulele

| D | D7 | G | A7 |

   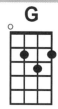

Baritone Ukulele

| D | D7 | G | A7 |

 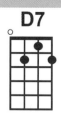  

Guitar

| D | D7 | G | A7 |

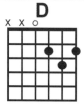  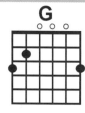 

Mandolin

| D | D7 | G | A7 |

 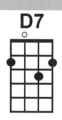  

Banjo

| D | D7 | G | A7 |

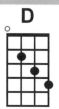 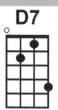 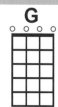 

Will the Circle Be Unbroken

Words by Ada R. Habershon
Music by Charles H. Gabriel

Standard Ukulele

G 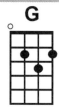   C 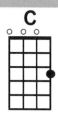   D7

Baritone Ukulele

G 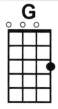   C    D7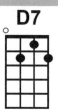

Guitar

G 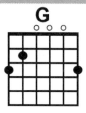   C 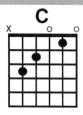   D7

Mandolin

G 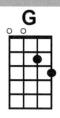   C 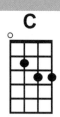   D7

Banjo

G 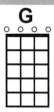   C 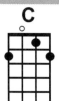   D7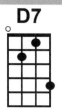

Worried Man Blues

Traditional

Standard Ukulele

C
C7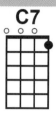
F
G7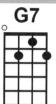

Baritone Ukulele

C
C7
F
G7

Guitar

C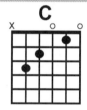
C7
F
G7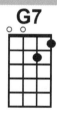

Mandolin

C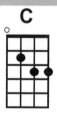
C7
F
G7

Banjo

C
C7
F
G7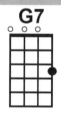

You Are My Sunshine

Words and Music by Jimmie Davis

Guitar Chord Songbooks

Each 6" x 9" book includes complete lyrics, chord symbols, and guitar chord diagrams.

Acoustic Hits
00701787 . . . . $14.99

Acoustic Rock
00699540 . . . . $22.99

Alabama
00699914 . . . . $14.95

The Beach Boys
00699566 . . . . $19.99

Bluegrass
00702585 . . . . $14.99

Johnny Cash
00699648 . . . . $19.99

Children's Songs
00699539 . . . . $17.99

Christmas Carols
00699536 . . . . $14.99

Christmas Songs
00119911 . . . . $14.99

Eric Clapton
00699567 . . . . $19.99

Classic Rock
00699598 . . . . $20.99

Coffeehouse Hits
00703318 . . . . $14.99

Country
00699534 . . . . $17.99

Country Favorites
00700609 . . . . $14.99

Country Hits
00140859 . . . . $14.99

Country Standards
00700608 . . . . $12.95

Cowboy Songs
00699636 . . . . $19.99

Creedence Clearwater Revival
00701786 . . . . $16.99

Jim Croce
00148087 . . . . $14.99

Crosby, Stills & Nash
00701609 . . . . $17.99

John Denver
02501697 . . . . $19.99

Neil Diamond
00700606 . . . . $22.99

Disney – 2nd Edition
00295786 . . . . $19.99

The Doors
00699888 . . . . $22.99

Eagles
00122917 . . . . $19.99

Early Rock
00699916 . . . . $14.99

Folksongs
00699541 . . . . $16.99

Folk Pop Rock
00699651 . . . . $17.99

40 Easy Strumming Songs
00115972 . . . . $16.99

Four Chord Songs
00701611 . . . . $16.99

Glee
00702501 . . . . $14.99

Gospel Hymns
00700463 . . . . $16.99

Grateful Dead
00139461 . . . . $17.99

Green Day
00103074 . . . . $17.99

Irish Songs
00701044 . . . . $16.99

Michael Jackson
00137847 . . . . $14.99

Billy Joel
00699632 . . . . $22.99

Elton John
00699732 . . . . $17.99

Ray LaMontagne
00130337 . . . . $12.99

Latin Songs
00700973 . . . . $14.99

Love Songs
00701043 . . . . $14.99

Bob Marley
00701704 . . . . $17.99

Bruno Mars
00125332 . . . . $12.99

Paul McCartney
00385035 . . . . $19.99

Steve Miller
00701146 . . . . $12.99

Modern Worship
00701801 . . . . $19.99

Motown
00699734 . . . . $19.99

Willie Nelson
00148273 . . . . $17.99

Nirvana
00699762 . . . . $17.99

Roy Orbison
00699752 . . . . $19.99

Peter, Paul & Mary
00103013 . . . . $19.99

Tom Petty
00699883 . . . . $17.99

Pink Floyd
00139116 . . . . $17.99

Pop/Rock
00699538 . . . . $19.99

Praise & Worship
00699634 . . . . $14.99

Elvis Presley
00699633 . . . . $17.99

Queen
00702395 . . . . $17.99

Red Hot Chili Peppers
00699710 . . . . $24.99

The Rolling Stones
00137716 . . . . $19.99

Bob Seger
00701147 . . . . $16.99

Carly Simon
00121011 . . . . $14.99

Sting
00699921 . . . . $24.99

Three Chord Acoustic Songs
00123860 . . . . $16.99

Three Chord Songs
00699720 . . . . $17.99

Two-Chord Songs
00119236 . . . . $16.99

U2
00137744 . . . . $19.99

Hank Williams
00700607 . . . . $16.99

Stevie Wonder
00120862 . . . . $14.99

Prices and availability subject to change without notice.

HAL•LEONARD®

Visit Hal Leonard online at **www.halleonard.com**